My wife, Janet, has been saying for some while that I should put my knowledge of Triumph Motor Cycles onto paper in the form of a book. To sit and produce a book is a daunting task, especially when the sunshine of New Zealand entices me outside to continue the restorations of my period Triumph machines, or to ride those which are restored, or at least road legal.

Having thought for a while, and it is not so painful as some would have you think, I decided that the most practical solution would be to possibly produce a series of booklets, instead of one large glossy book. This would have many advantages for both myself and those who might be sufficiently interested to purchase such previously unpublished information on Triumph motor cycles; and goodness knows enough books have been published on the subject in the previous few years, with errors replicated, not to mention the incomplete and inaccurate Triumph dating sheets of which no one knows the original source.

Among the advantages are the necessity for me to only sit for relatively short periods indoors in front of the computer screen; I would be able to publish and distribute smaller booklets without too much, if any, outside assistance and expense; smaller books equate to smaller overheads and therefore lower cost to prospective readers and postal handling would similarly be smaller; prospective purchasers would not have to lay out large sums of money for a large book, of which maybe only certain pages were of interest, for they could purchase just the booklet, or booklets, of specific interest if they did not wish to collect the whole series; and finally, if I should fall off my perch before the task is through at least some of the knowledge I have obtained over the years will have been made available to fellow enthusiasts.

Thus, to my wife Janet, my series of books is dedicated

Edition details

COPYRIGHT © 2024

Published by

Published by Richard Cornelius
ISBN 978-1-915382-09-2
www.earlytriumph.com
A catalogue version is available at The British Library

This edition

Eighth edition – April 2024

Significant changes and formatting due to re-publishing via modern global distribution methods after being entrusted to his son, Richard Cornelius.
There are some minor additions to update the information for the new version, plus amendments to some of the wording for contextual reasons, including the book title, though as much as possible the text has remained identical to the original version (edition 7) from Peter Cornelius. If there are any errors that may have been introduced by this process, these are unintentional and please let us know via www.earlytriumph.com
To ensure that the images, most of which are original from the early 20th century, retain as much detail as possible, it has been determined that although costlier, a higher quality than usual printing process is specified.
Updated and published by Richard Cornelius, son of the original author, Peter Cornelius.

Previous editions

First edition - 2001

First published and distributed public edition. Created, published, and distributed by Peter Cornelius

Second edition - 2006

Second Edition updated, published, and distributed by Peter Cornelius. Changes include:
Contents Page; Page 10 - The tank hand-pump connection is NOT to the front of the crankcase, as the earlier Model P. The feed pipe goes to the oil pump at the rear of the crankcase; Page 22 - The Primary Chain size to read, 5/8 inch X 1/4 inch, 52 links

Third edition - May 2011

Third Edition of the Triumph Models N, NP and QA-2 booklet has only very minor additions from previous Editions, but the opportunity has been taken to standardise the caption fonts with other booklets in this series. Updated, published, and distributed by Peter Cornelius

Fourth edition - 2014

Updated, published, and distributed by Peter Cornelius

Fifth edition - May 2015

Updated, published, and distributed by Peter Cornelius

Sixth edition – April 2018

Sixth Edition has only very minor additions from the previous three Editions
Updated, published, and distributed by Peter Cornelius

Seventh edition - January 2020

Seventh Edition has corrections of conflicting information regarding tank lining and wheel rim finishes.
Updated, published, and distributed by Peter Cornelius

Triumph 1927-1928, Models N, NP and QA-2

Contents

Introduction

Models N, NP and QA

The 1927 Model N was a logical progression from the very successful 494cc 1925/26 Model P. Basically the same engine was used with the addition of an internal "semi-automatic" oil pump along with the later evolvement of the Model P gearbox. These were placed into an updated frame with Webb single-spring forks and a brake-shoe rear hub replaced the long-used dummy belt-rim brake. The single internal band front brake remained but beaded edge tyres disappeared for ever and wired-on rims and tyres were fitted. A few other minor changes but hey presto a Model N, and another success story for Triumph.

Initially announced as the Model 'N de Luxe' this was to later lead to confusion when for 1928 the machine was modernised to have a saddle tank and the updated machine was known as the 'N de Luxe', while the 'N' continued for the 1928 season but was listed as the Model NP. Consequentially in order to avoid confusion the 1927 machine has become more commonly known as the straight 'Model N' and that is the reference I shall use in this book; while the 1928-29 saddle tank Model N de Luxe is the subject of a separate book.

The Model QA came in two varieties; hence my non-official naming of 'QA-2' in the book title. In 1926 a Sports version of the Model P was announced - the Model Q, and also a Super Sports - the Model QA. However, the 1926 Model QA owed more to its Model P ancestry than the Model QA of 1927, which was the sports version of the Model N. Thus this book will relate only factors relative to the **1927** Model of the QA.

A comfortable ride.
The Brooks Supple Seat fitted to these models is easily identified by the radiating flat springs coupled to the rather delicate springs around the rear of the frame.

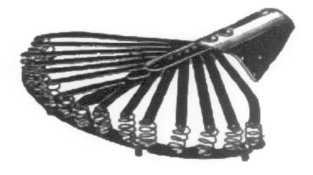

▷	N	1927
▷	QA	1927
▷	NP	1928

Brief Details

The Model N was an update of the Model P, with a built-in automatic oil pump, a heavier frame, an aluminium piston and wired-on tyres.

▷   494cc (493.2cc) Side Valve Engine
▷   84mm bore X 89mm stroke
▷   Compression Ratio

     N   4.5:1
     NP   4.5:1
     QA   4.75:1

▷   3 Speed

     Solo   5.06, 8.2 & 14.12 to 1
     Sidecar 5.46, 8.85 & 15.2 to 1

▷   Multiple Dry Plate Clutch
▷   All chain drive
▷   Tyres

     Home market   27 X 2.75 Wired-on tyres (26 X 3.25 was extra £1-10-0)
     Overseas   26 X 3.25 Wired-on tyres

▷   Ground clearance - 4 1/2 inches
▷   Weight

     N   250 lbs
     NP   250 lbs
     QA   244 lbs

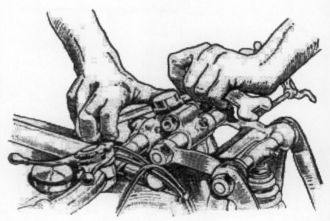

Adjusting the steering head.

This picture also shows the twin-lever throttle and air controls with their distinctive notched friction adjusters of the period.

Listed Prices

(Home Market unless specified otherwise)

1927

Model N	£45- 0-0
	£73- 5-0 in New Zealand
	£91- 0-0 in New Zealand
	Down to £70- 0-0 in December
	1125 Reich Marks in Germany Model
Model QA	£48-10-0

1928

Model NP	£42-17-6 initially
	£45-17-6
	£75- 0-0 in New Zealand

Extras

Acetylene lamps & bulb horn	£2-10-0
Magdyno, lights & bulb horn	£5-15-0
Rear carrier (Model QA)	£1- 0-0
Twist grip control (Amac)	£1- 0-0
Footboards	£1- 0-0
Touring Handlebars	No charge
26 X 3.25 tyres	£1-10-0

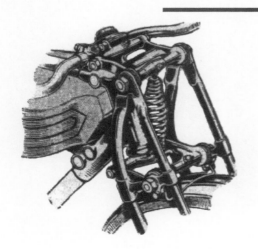

The new-for-1927
single-spring Webb forks

Identification Features / Variations

- Spark plug mounted in head, between valve caps
- Triumph mechanical oil pump with circular sight glass in crankcase (see Technicalities chapter)
- Triumph semi-automatic twin-barrel carburettor
- Gearbox has combined filler/level plug mounted at an angle on rear surface of casing (see Technicalities chapter)
- Fuel tank
    - Flat tank
    - Tank top raised along centre line
    - 2 inches outside diameter screw-fitting fuel and oil caps
    - Fuel capacity 1 3/4 gallons
    - Oil capacity 2 pints
    - Oil handpump on right-hand side of tank, rear of filler cap
    - Single oil outlet
    - Tap in oil feed line and part of hand pump assembly
    - Crest transfer on tank sides
- Gold trumpet and crest transfers on frame headstock
- Single tension spring front forks
- Handlebar clamps from the rear of forks
- Standard handlebars with open ended levers
- Exhaust-valve lifter lever mounted with clutch lever
- Twin-lever throttle and air controls on right-hand of bars
- Single lever on left of bars for magneto advance/retard
- Throttle twist grip optional extra; in which case a left mounted twin lever controls magneto and air
- Brakes
    - Front Brake 6" semi-servo internal expanding band
    - Rear Brake 7" twin expanding shoe
- Exhaust
    - Had the 'finned egg' primary silencer, in addition to the -
    - Standard silencer
    - The tailpipe ends with a large fishtail
- Tyre inflator mounted under lower cross-tube of frame
- The optional bulb horn would have been a Lucas No. 63

Model N

> ⊳ Tank
>> French Grey,
>> with Green panels,
>> outlined gold,
>> overall red lining
> ⊳ Rear carrier standard fitting with single toolbox over mudguard at rear
> ⊳ Wheel rims
>> The sales brochure stated that there were plated edges to wheel rims, with black centre and no lining. However, all pictures show total black rims and spokes, with gold lining on the rims
> ⊳ Brooks Supple Seat B.190/1c

Model QA

> ⊳ Tank
>> French Grey,
>> with Green panels,
>> outlined gold,
>> overall red lining
> ⊳ Much additional Nickel Plating
>> exhaust system
>> both chaincovers
>> front brakeplate
>> fork links
>> rear chain sprocket
>> footrests
> ⊳ All aluminium parts highly polished
>> including crankcase and gearbox
> ⊳ Carrier not standard. (£1-0-0 optional extra.)
> ⊳ Single toolbox mounted low down on the left-hand rear mudguard stays
> ⊳ Wheel rims plated edges, black centre, red lining
> ⊳ Brooks Supple Seat B.190/1c

Model NP

> ⊳ Tank
>> Black
>> Saxe Blue (light blue) panelled
>> gold lined
> ⊳ Rear carrier standard fitting with single toolbox over mudguard at rear
> ⊳ Wheels rims all-black and gold lined
> ⊳ Special Terry Saddle (in catalogue) or Brooks B.189 (in Parts List)

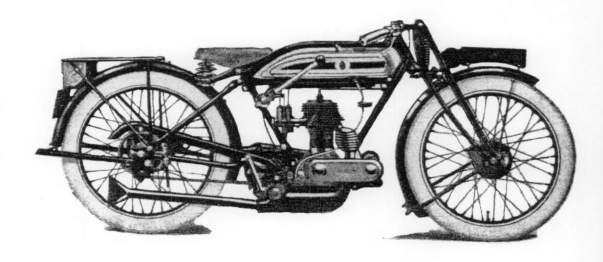

Spot the differences

Above is the 1927 Model N and below is the Model QA from the same year, 1927.

Having both together makes it easier to see differences between the models, such as the additional nickel plating, no rear carrier as standard on the QA, and subsequent change of location for the toolbox

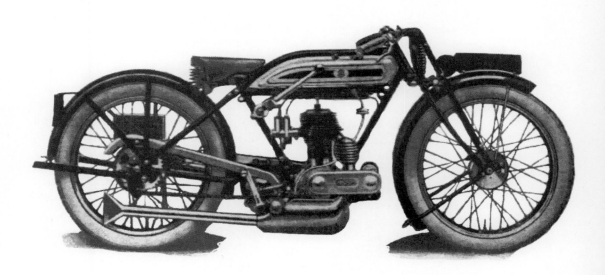

Background
to the Triumph Models N, NP and QA

By the mid 1920s Triumph, along with most other motor cycle manufacturers, were in financial trouble. Profits of £41,546 for the year 1922/23 had dropped to £32,822 for 1923/24. The introduction of assembly line manufacturing and a low unit-profit product, the 1925 Model P, had returned Triumph to being a successful business, while many others 'went to the wall'. (Low profit success? Better to sell 1,000 items with a profit of £1 on each, than 100 items with a profit of £5 on each. Herbert Austin did the same thing when he dropped the price of the Austin Seven by £100.)

While the Model P was selling by the 10,000 Triumph were looking at further ways to cash in on its success. The first step was to make a Sports version of the Model P, the Model Q. The 1926 Model Q was for the home market only and a Model QA (Q Advanced?), was the Overseas Super Sports machine, although it was also available in limited quantities on the home market.

For the 1927 season Triumph introduced an improved Model P - the Model N. Although it boasted "semi-automatic" engine lubrication, single-spring Webb forks, modern rear drum brake and wired-on tyres many of its components were identical to those of the Model P or subtly changed to incur no additional manufacturing costs. Thus Triumph were still able to maintain high reliability, loyalty from their customers, and profits for their shareholders.

Since the 1926 sports Models Q and QA had also been popular it made sense to also have a sports version of the Model N. I guess to continue its recognition by the customers the sports version was still to be known as the Model QA. It's just unfortunate for us, 74 years later, that there were two machines of the same name which were different in many important aspects. (The Vintage Motor Cycle Club needs we Marque Specialists to identify things like this!)

Although the Models N and QA were very popular and sold well, 'the times they were a changing'. For 1928 the Model N took a further step forward and with a new frame adopted a saddle tank and separate oil tank - the Model N de Luxe. Being much lower and appearing more sportsman like there was no need for a separate sports model and the Model QA disappeared from the sales catalogue. In fact a number of models disappeared from the catalogue for the then Managing Director, Colonel Claude Vivian Holbrook, was concentrating on car sales and there were but four models listed for 1928; however some deficiencies in the product line were rectified by announcements in April 1928.
Along with the saddle tank Model N de Luxe for 1928 the Model N was continued, but in recognition of its inheritance it was called the Model NP! Although changes were absolutely minimal it had a very different look about it; for the French Grey with Brunswick Green of the tank, which had been Triumph's colours since late 1913, changed to the new colours of Black with Blue panels.

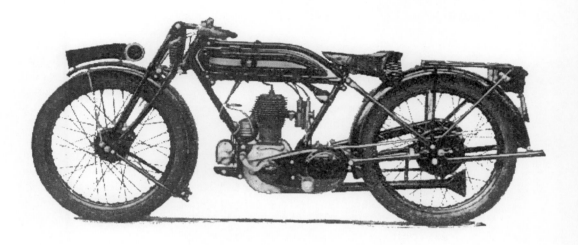

The 1928 Model NP with gold lined blue panelled tank.
Everything else which wasn't nickelled was black!

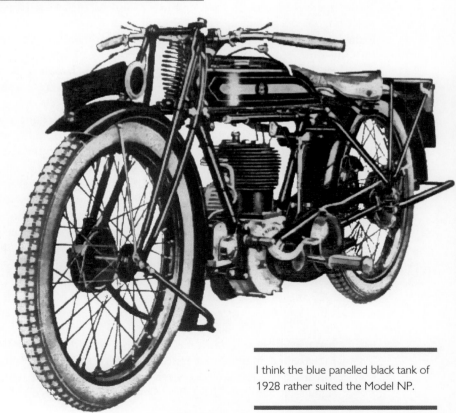

I think the blue panelled black tank of
1928 rather suited the Model NP.

Notes

on the Models N, QA and NP

The Models N and QA were announced at the same time in September, 1926. To give it the 'sporty' look the Model QA had much more nickel plating and the alloy crankcase and gearbox were highly polished. To give it 'the edge' on performance, or at least give the impression of, the compression was slightly greater and the engine ports were smoothed and polished.

The engine and gearbox were basically that of the Model P, with its semi-turbulent head to give maximum efficiency with even fuel burn, the crankshaft running in double-ball bearings and the connecting rod big-end with roller bearings. The valves were of cobalt chrome steel and the gears of the gearbox were of high tensile nickel-chrome steel. Gear selector forks were changed from the earlier malleable castings to heat-treated steel stampings.

By 1926 the general public were becoming quite irate concerning the noise made by motor cycles and in August that year the police were directed to take stern action against noisy motorcycles and fines were to be increased to a maximum of £10 instead of the standard £1 or £2.
Many standard machines did not meet the required silencing level and riders were being fined even though they had not modified their machines at all. The law regarding silencing simply said, "He (the motor owner) shall not use a cut-out, fitting, or any other apparatus or device, which will allow the gases ... to escape into the atmosphere without first passing through a silencer, expansion chamber, or other contrivance, suitable and sufficient for reducing as far as may be reasonably practical the noise which would otherwise be caused by the escape of the said gases." This Law dated from the end of 1912.
The Model P is not the quietest of machines, in fact it has quite a bark which even today still has horses rearing in fright. So after six months of experimentation Triumph came up with the additional primary silencer as fitted to these three 1927 models. I call it the 'finned egg', but call it what you will it couldn't have been very successful as it lasted but a few years. Being of two pressed halves of thin sheet it must have suffered badly from the heat of the exhaust gases. Even without such a device the Model P silencer is prone to burning through where the gasses are turned about six inches further on from where this primary device was fitted. Very few surviving machines have been found to have this primary silencer fitted, for over the years the plain Model P type pipe has replaced it.

From 1925 the British Army relied heavily upon the Model P, in both solo and sidecar trim and these were supplemented by 1927 Models N, 1928 Models NP and 1929 Models NL. The Motor Cycle for 16th June 1927 said that the War Office had placed an order with the Triumph Company for a number of machines. This was actually late news as twenty nine Models N had been taken into Army service on June 1st, 1927. These were put into daily service with the Armoured Force Signals on Salisbury Plain. They subsequently averaged 900 miles a month

(10,800 miles a year) and none went into the workshops on account of a mechanical breakdown. The Despatch Rider timetables showed that they averaged over 47 mph. They were used in the Southern Command Tattoo, jumping 35 to 40 feet without affecting frame or forks. They were also used at the Royal Tournament at Olympia.

Although the Model NP was not listed for 1929 it was, in fact, still being manufactured in order to satisfy a Government contract for the Army. Contract C1412 was drawn up on the 20th December 1928 and machines were still being registered by the Army up until mid 1929.

The Corporal looks happy with his sidecar hauling Model NP as this was one of the last from Coventry, for the registration indicates mid-1929.

The rear mounted oil pump and sight glass of the Models N, NP and QA.

The oil feed to the crankcase differs between these flat-tank models and the later saddle-tank models. Note that the oil feed to the mechanical oil pump is made via a single banjo connection.

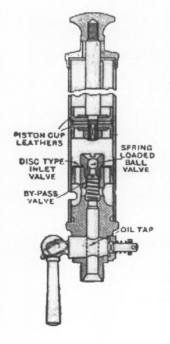

PISTON CUP LEATHERS

DISC TYPE INLET VALVE

BY-PASS VALVE

SPRING LOADED BALL VALVE

OIL TAP

Note the by-pass valve in the tank hand-pump to allow oil to flow direct to the crankcase pump. The tap is to prevent oil overfilling the automatic pump when parked up for a long period as it can pass through the pump and fill the crankcase! Remember to turn on when running!

The official documentation of the period is inconsistent in how the oil pipe is routed.

Looking again at the picture on the previous page (an image taken from the instruction book), it shows the pipe neatly behind the tappets, however if you choose this route ensure that it does not touch anything which could cause abrasion of the pipe;

The picture to the right (an official Model QA picture), has the pipe very 'free' and liable to damage, in fact it doesn't show any antivibration turns in the pipe, which if not included will cause problems as plated pipes are brittle.

The correct routing is displayed in the sales images (see the pictures in the previous chapter "Identification Features/Variations"), being under the primary silencer and outside of the tappets.

It may not have escaped your notice that the previous official picture does not show the primary silencer!

Shown here the primary silencer can be clearly seen as two-half pressings.
There were actually TWO versions, as the 'for use with magdyno' version needed an indentation to clear the dynamo!

The Models N, above, and QA, below, from the 1927 Australian sales catalogue.
The 26 X 3.25 tyres give an altogether different look to the machines.

Note in the top picture the mounting of the battery carrier when electric lights
were fitted.
(Note also; the Colonials were not bothered by noise antagonists - no primary
silencers!)

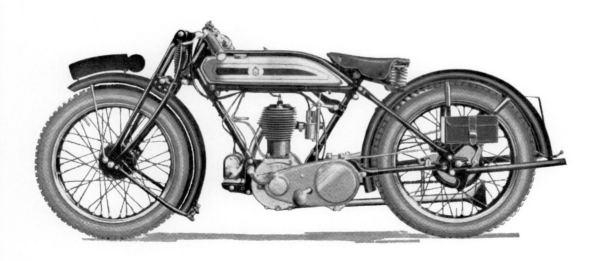

Competition Successes

Despite their short production life the Models N and QA earned a number of competitive successes; particularly in the hands of lady rider Edyth Foley. Edyth had previously ridden a Model P and with the new models excelled and achieved many successes and put many a man to shame. In a number of instances she was obviously Model QA mounted, which makes sense since that was the 'sportsperson's' model, although in other instances only the engine size was quoted and we cannot presume that she always had a Model QA. Since she was such a successful rider one can assume that she was supplied with a machine from the Triumph Works, although she probably didn't work there. (At one time Triumph proudly advertised that, "We employ no women!" although things were changing and ladies such as Edyth Foley was showing that they were well the equal of men, and some obviously more equal! In fact the statement wasn't true when it was made as ladies were employed in the office and at this time things were changing so rapidly that by 1929 ladies/girls were watching over up to eight automatic turret lathes in the Triumph Works. But I digress. Another subject for another book.)

Edyth got off to an early start in 1927 on a Model QA by winning the Alan Douglas Trophy for the best performance of any machine and the Harvey Kelly Trophy for the best solo performance in the 1927 Southport Coast to Coast Trial. (300 miles; Southport - Scarborough - Southport, without loss of points.)

The Six Days Standard Stock Machine Trial was a test of 'stock standard' machines. Held in May 1927 over 750 miles of varying terrain the Triumph Team were Edyth Foley, Wilmot Evans and Fred Edmond. Each won a Gold Medal for finishing without the loss of a single point and they also won a Team Award. Miss Foley was described as, "being almost out of reach of the ground and not looking at all comfortable, but made a faultless (but not footless) performance."
Evans and Edmond were reported as being, "Two powerful riders who found their utmost skill necessary on occasion. Although the Model Ns handled coarsely there was no question of their power and excellent final condition."

Miss Edyth Foley won a further Gold Medal in the Scottish Six Days Trial during July 1927; 494cc Triumph and probably again the Model QA.

In the August 1927 International Six Days Trial Triumph tied for the Class C, 500cc, Manufacturers Team award but it was awarded to the team having the smaller engines. Miss Edyth Foley on the Model QA was a member of the ladies team which won the International Silver Vase for England. Triumph mounted riders gained four Gold Medals in the 1927 ISDT.

Miss Edith Foley rode a Model QA in
the 1927 Southport Coast to Coast
Trial

The Triumph team for the 1927 Six Days Standard Stock
Machine Trial. Left to right are Wilmot Evans, Edyth Foley and
F.G. Edmond.
Although described as "de Luxe Model Ns", Evans and Foley
appear to be Model QA mounted while Edmond seems to have
a Model N.

Miss Edyth Foley takes a break for a Horlicks malted milk on her Model QA during the 1927 Six Days Standard Stock Machine Trial. May 1927

The Model QA still performing sterling service under the guidance of Miss Edyth Foley as a member of the ladies team which won the International Silver Vase for England in the 1927 International Six Days Trial

Edyth now with her crash hat, ready for a go at dirt track riding!
The Models N and QA also make excellent normal road machines!

Sales and Production Figures

This is still the subject of my researches and therefore not yet complete. It is not easy to determine accurate production figures by model, for despite the addition of the crankcase oil pump engines continued to be numbered in the Model P/Q/QA-1 series and for the home market Model P production continued for a while into 1927, while Models N and QA-2 commenced construction in September 1926. So there were overlaps of the different engines being constructed while being numbered irrespective of with, or without, oil pump. Likewise gearboxes were common across the range.

Only Models N, QA-2 and NP used the 10xxxxx series frame, so this assists to a degree.

Models N and QA production appears to have finished in October 1927, while Model NP started in November 1927 but may not have gone beyond March 1928. From my researches to date it would appear that in total something in the order of 10,000 to 12,000 Models N and QA-2 were built. Around 3,000 of these were made during the last months of 1926. (When declaring the age of your machine for rallies, etc., do use the manufacture date, rather than the 'model year'; because that's how old it really is. The Models N and QA-2 may only have been catalogued for 1927, but at least a quarter of them were made in the previous year.)

Many of these early production machines were shipped overseas - mainly to Australia, Triumph's largest export market, and New Zealand on the same shipping route - so that they could be available around the same time as the home market models.

I would approximate that around 1,500 to 2,000 of these N & QAs would have been of the Model QA version.

Total Model NP production would appear to have been around the 1,800 figure, with something in the order of 600 made in 1927 and 1,200 in 1928.

Sales

It was quite common for end of season models to be reduced in price when the following year models were announced. This was generally about a 12% reduction. However, in October and November 1927 the 1927 N model was being advertised at £38, which was a slightly above average 15.5% reduction and was probably due to the fact that its replacement in the 1928 line was a modern saddle-tank model and the Model N continuation, NP, was to sell at £2-2-6 less than the 1927 model had been sold for.

Technicalities

Lubrication

The Triumph mechanical oil pump in the crankcase has a lever marked "On/Off". Actually it is not an on/off switch, but an oil feed adjuster which may be set at intermediate positions. To quote from the 1926 announcement of the Model W, which had the same pump:-

"Lubrication is by a neat self-contained mechanical pump, the rotor of which is driven by skew gears from the crankshaft. In the end of the rotor is a small plunger which is carried around with the main body. Its reciprocating action is controlled by a stationary pin, the eccentricity of which to the centre of the rotor is variable."

(I'm not sure that I understand the last sentence - but it can obviously be varied!)

At the bottom of the oil pump reservoir are cast the letters "DRY" which just might be seen through the sight glass if the oil stops flowing from the oil tank. (The tightening of the engine will probably indicate this condition before those three letters are discerned!)

The Model N de Luxe of 1928 had differences associated with the oil pump. As far as I can ascertain the Model NP engine appears to have also had these improvements incorporated; while still maintaining the Model P/N engine number sequence. These small differences included the following:-

The central boss on drive-side
▷   Model N has a leather oil seal
▷   Model NP may have a grooved oil slinger/thrower

The oil pump non-return valve
▷   Model N has one
▷   Model NP may not

For 1928, in order to improve the visibility of the oil flow in the sight feed a small spout was incorporated.

Most Models N, QA and NP have the gearbox with the combined filler/level plug mounted at an angle on rear surface of casing, but it is quite possible that the early Models N and QA had the Model P style 'froth-tower' oil filler. These two different gearbox casings were numbered in the same sequence. The inability to overfill the gearbox was claimed to entirely eliminate clutch-slip problems. This, unfortunately, is not so.

Terry's kick start replacement spring was a K54, which is 1 1/4 inches o/d with 8 coil turns of SWG 10 wire (0.128 inches, 3.24mm); nickel plated.

Triumph frames were coslettised, which is a corrosion-protective treatment for the steel. Originated by the English chemist Coslett it consists of boiling the frame in a solution of phosphoric acid in order that a phosphate coating be formed on the surface of the steel. It was very effective and few frames are found today in an irrecoverable condition. Today I use Jenolite; a modern liquid which is basically phosphoric acid.

The mudguards are 5 inches wide.

The wheel rim lining (Models QA and NP) is approx. 3/32 inch wide, on each side, half-way between the outer edge of rim & central raised portion but do not be too concerned as remember that originally this was all hand done so there were bound to be variations between machines.

Fuel Tank

1927
Petrol tank colour; BS 381C (1964) French Grey.
The Green Panel is "Brunswick Green".
The Red is "Post Office Red".
The gold lining around the green panels is approx. 3/32 inch wide while the overall red outline is around 1/16 inch wide but do not be too concerned as remember that originally this was all hand done so there were bound to be variations between tanks.

1928
Petrol tank colour; Saxe Blue, apparently equates to a Sky/Pale Blue.
For the Blue "Humbrol No.48" was acceptable, but I don't have an alternative to the Humbrol number though an owner from NSW, Australia, has found that Storm Blue from the Australian Coloryte colour guide A.S 2700 1997 edition is close to my Humbrol No.48 recommendation for the tank.
Gold lined around panels, approx. 3/32 inch wide while the overall gold outline is approx. 1/16 inch wide but do not be too concerned as remember that originally this was all hand done so there were bound to be variations between tanks.

Craftmaster at www.craftmasterpaints.co.uk/colours-standard-range.htm have also been recommended, since Humbrol colours are no longer reliable.

The tank fuel/oil caps were made by Rotherham and Sons Ltd. of Coventry and carry the engraving "R Y S". They are 2 inches outer diameter and approx. 1 7/8 inch internal diameter with a 20tpi thread.

Note the raised centre rib on the tank.
This and the single oil outlet distinguish
the tank of the Models N, QA and NP.

Note also that while the fuel tank side panels and
lining terminate at the rear to a point, the overall
outer lining terminates with a 'cut-off'. This is very
often not noticed by those repainting the tank.
The 'cut-off' was a left-over from the earlier
Models H & SD whose tanks terminated with a
'cut-off'. Triumph's lining man simply carried the
practice on even though the tanks themselves
now terminated to a point.

Engine

The alloy piston of the Models N,
QA and NP. Note the cutaway sides
and split in the skirt.

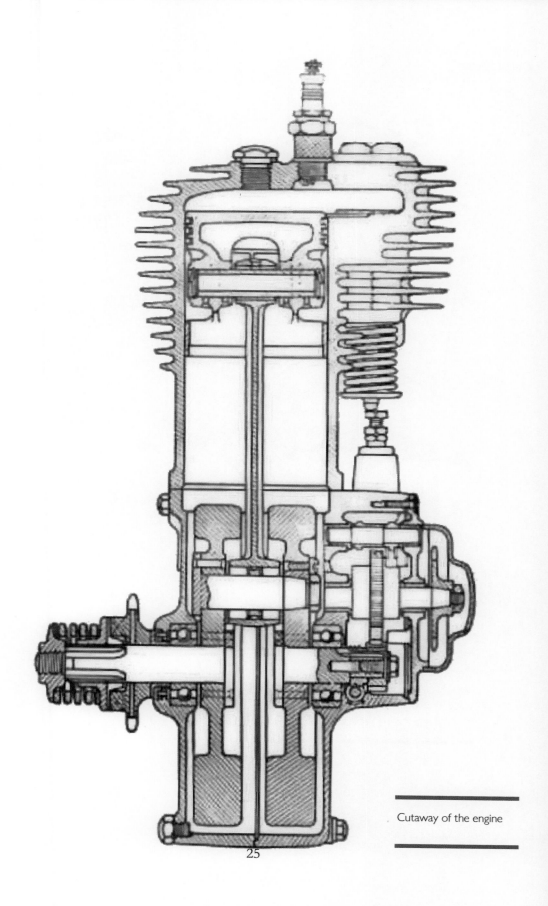

Cutaway of the engine

Carburetter

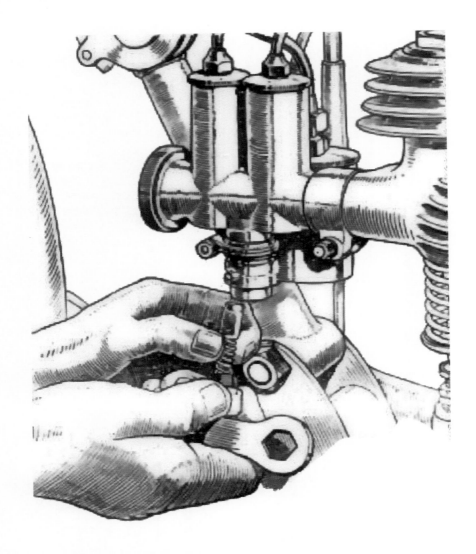

The Triumph twin-barrel carburetter (period
spelling) which had given such reliable service and
economy since 1915, on almost all models.
1928 was to be the last year of its use.

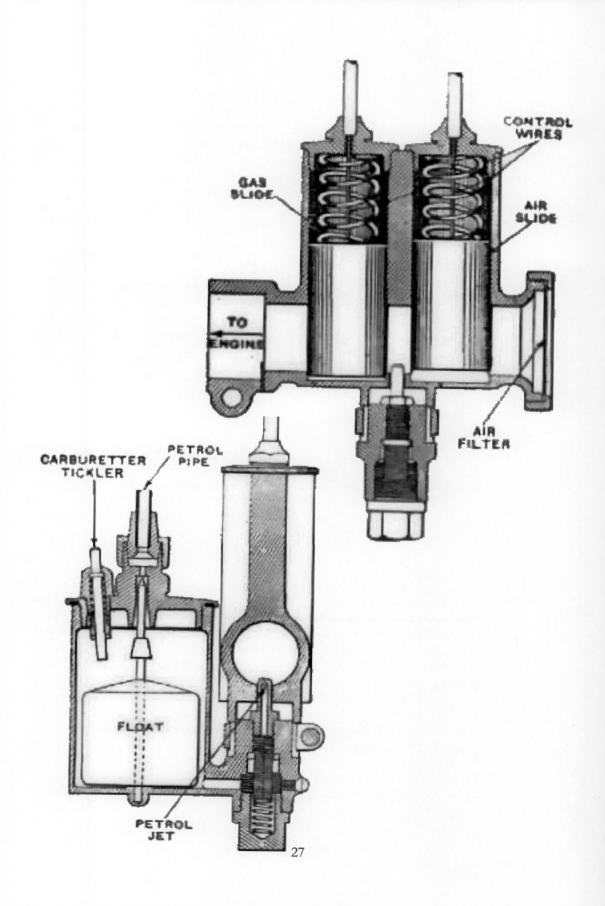

CONTROL WIRES

GAS SLIDE

AIR SLIDE

TO ENGINE

AIR FILTER

CARBURETTER TICKLER

PETROL PIPE

FLOAT

PETROL JET

27

Clutch

Clutch friction plates were 5 inches o/d X 4 inches i/d X 1/10th inch thick.
Clutch steel plates were also 1/10th inch thick.
The clutch pushrod is 7/32 inch Diam. X 7 11/16 inches to 8 inches long.

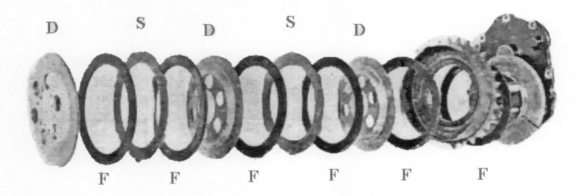

Do note the sequence of clutch plate assembly.
This is critical, and pictures in the Triumph sales literature are incorrect!

       F = a Fibre plate
       S = a Steel plate
       D = a Dished plate (dishing raised away from gearbox)

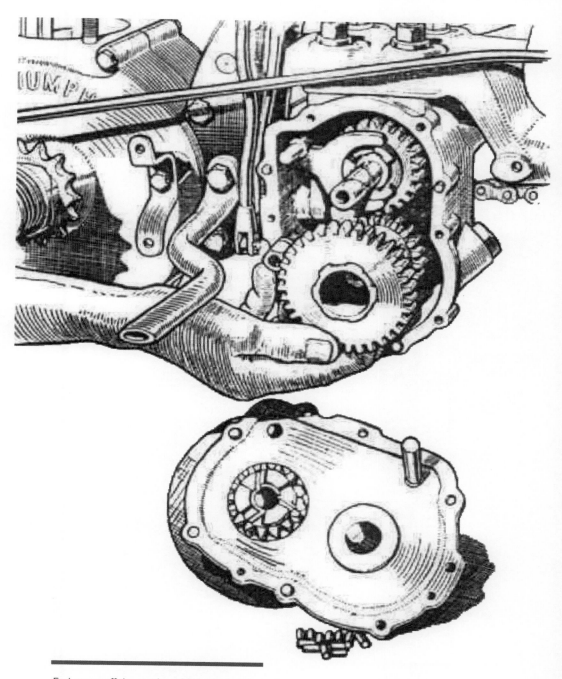

End cover off the gearbox. Note the bend
in the gearchange linkage and the angled
filler cum level plug.

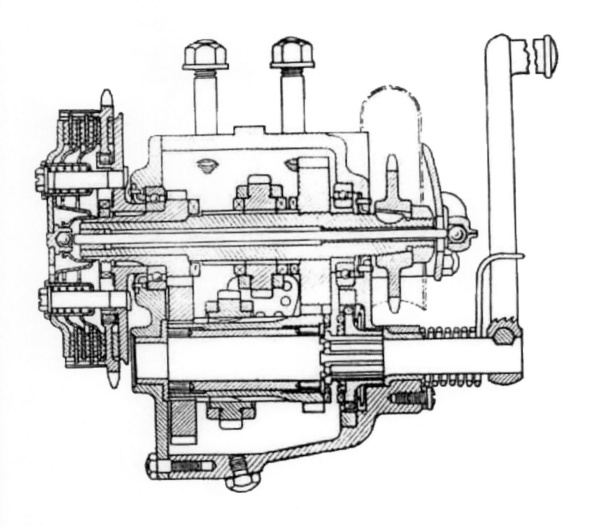

Cutaway of the gearbox and clutch.

The throttle/air and advance/retard control levers were made under a James Doherty of Birmingham patent. By the time of the Model N de Luxe there was individual adjustment for the levers and this is most apparent from the four C-spanner insertion places on the upper surface circumference.

Chains and Bearings

The magneto chain is 1/2 inch x 1/8th inch. 44 links.
The primary chain is 5/8 inch x 1/4th inch, 52 links.
The rear chain is 5/8th inch x 1/4 inch. 89 links, solo. 92 links, sidecar.
Taper front and rear wheel bearings have 9 rollers and are stamped W5386.

Electrics

The magneto was a Lucas KSA1.
The magdyno was a Lucas MDB1.

A Note on the Engine Lubrication

These models, and the more common Model N in particular, are likely to be a first vintage motor cycle for newcomers more accustomed to modern recirculating or sump oil lubrication systems so a word might not go amiss regarding the total loss system and Triumph's "semi-automatic" oil pump.

Initially with a new or overhauled engine four pumps with the hand pump supplies sufficient oil to the crankcase to be splashed around by the flywheel and lubricate bearings and piston. While running, some oil will get past the piston and be burnt off while much more will seep out of the primitive oil seals. There is no recirculation of the oil. (Triumph didn't introduce this until 1929; on other models.) To replace this lost oil from the crankcase it was previously customary to give one pump of the hand pump every 10 miles, or a half a pump every 5 miles.

The new for 1927 oil pump doesn't supply oil under pressure. It simply continually drip feeds to keep the crankcase adequately supplied without the need to remember to pump every 5 or 10 miles.

The Triumph mechanical oil pump was/is quite adequate for maintaining the crankcase oil but as the concept of automatic oiling was new, the hand pump was retained as a sop to conservative owners who understood that the hand pump pushed oil and had difficulty in coming to terms with the new-fangled automatic device. Triumph's instructions were that the hand pump could be used if it was felt to be necessary!

LUCAS "Magdyno" Lighting and Ignition System.

Diagram of Wiring for TRIUMPH Models "N" & "QA."

Diagram shows switch in "off" position, which provides half dynamo charge with lights off.

With switch in "C" position, E is connected to S, and L to T, giving full dynamo charge and lights off.

With switch in "L" position, E is connected to S, and L to T and + D, giving full dynamo charge, low light and tail light.

With switch in "H" position, E is connected to S, and T to + D and H, giving full charge, high light and tail light.

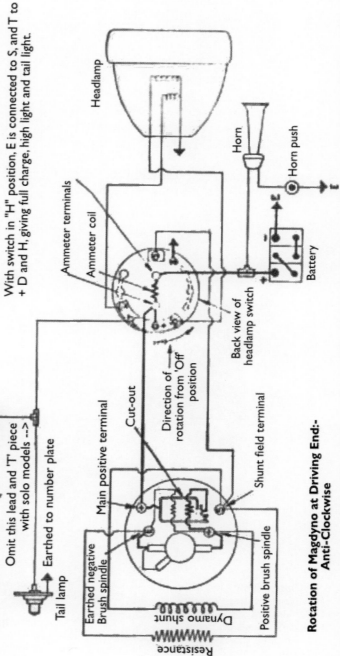

Rotation of Magdyno at Driving End:- Anti-Clockwise

Known Problems

There is a tendency for the exhaust valve to stick open if the engine is over oiled. The driven splines on the end of the internal oil pump tend to wear over the years. The dogs in the gearbox may wear, causing jumping out of middle gear. Surface grinding of the dogs can give a temporary cure. Gearbox Middle Gears are the ones which tend to take any mistreatment. The two gears affected are P/N 6151 Layshaft Middle Gear Wheel (28 teeth) and P/N 6146 Mainshaft Middle Gear Wheel (24 teeth).

A slipping clutch may result from oil leakage from the gearbox mainshaft. It may also be due to a worn mainshaft bearing, the leather washer inside the gearbox, or excess oil breathing from the engine.

The main silencer burns through at the lower front, where the gases are suddenly turned through near 90 degrees.

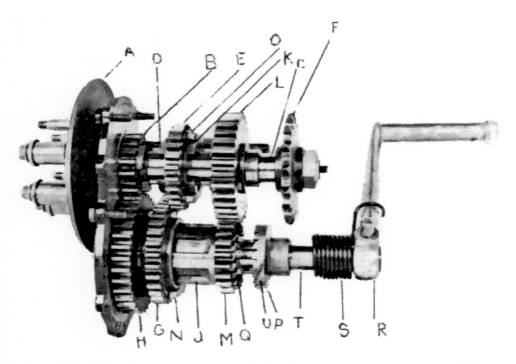

A. Clutch driving member	G. Layshaft middle gear wheel	Q. Ratchet on layshaft low gear wheel
B. Constant mesh pinion	H Constant mesh wheel	R. Kick-starter crank
C. Mainshaft	I. Layshaft	S. Kick-starter crank spring
D. and K. Dogs on mainshaft middle gear wheel	L. Mainshaft low gear wheel	T. Kick-starter axle
E. Mainshaft middle gear wheel	M. Layshaft low gear wheel	U. Lug on ratchet sleeve
F. Rear chain sprocket	N. and O. Selector forks	
	P. Kick-starter ratchet sleeve.	
	F. Rear chain sprocket	

Original spark plug was Lodge Type TS3. Suitable sparking plugs (18mm, 1/2" reach) are; Lodge H1, Champion 17, Champion D16, Bosch DM165 and KLG M60.

I understand that some 2 litre, four cylinder car pistons fit these engines. Unfortunately I have no specific details, but believe these are the Mark 2 Ford Zepher piston.

I am also given to understand that a 500cc Royal Enfield Bullet piston is a perfect alternative. This one is believed to be Hepolite 7250, but has not been confirmed. Model N valves are 11/32 inch (0.34375 in.) diameter. BSA M20 valves (0.354) may be made to fit.

Diesel engine valves are superior to motorcycle types. Part number believed to be TRW 105/33981.

Valve springs appear to be 2.5 inches length, unmounted, and 1.25 inches diameter made up of 8 turns of 0.128 inch diameter (SWG 10) wire.

I do not recommend that you plate springs. The plating process causes "hydrogen embrittlement" which can result in fracturing or breaking. In order to prevent this it is necessary to expel that hydrogen and this can only be achieved by heating the plated item to a very high temperature WITHIN 2 HOURS of the completion of the plating. I don't think that anyone, anywhere, would find a plating company with such facilities today. A spray with silver paint would be the safest action today. You have been warned! Triumph never plated their fork springs, possibly because they could not guarantee removal of all the hydrogen resulting from the plating process and didn't want claims for accidents due to broken springs.

Main bearings were MC22 of 50 X 22 X 17mm. Originally these were double-row self-aligning so if you have originals which are usable stick with them. A Spanish made MC22 is available, but of single row. Cheaper SKF 50 X 22 X 14mm bearings, Part No. 62/22, also single row, may be used with a 3mm spacer turned to fit the crankcase prior to the bearing, keeping the bearings close to the crank assembly.

If you have crankshaft problems I am advised that the Model P crankshaft may be turned down, without dismantling the flywheels, to accept the drive for the oil pump on the Models N, QA and NP. (Not actually done but it was noted that other dimensions were the same.)

The carburettor float needle is 3.0665 inches long with 1.3025 inches above the float and 0.315 inches below.

It is common for oil to leak from the gearbox. I personally use SAE 140 oil or a mixture of SAE 140 and Penrite semi-liquid grease.

If you are using an earlier Model P gearbox which has no level plug, do not attempt to drill and tap as the gearbox shell is too thin to support more than about 1½ threads!

The two gearbox roller bearings (P/N 6144) are 54mm o/d, 28.5mm i/d, 9.5mm wide. (2 1/8 X 1 1/8 X 3/8 inches). I purchased March 2005 under a product code R18.

Suggested correct tension for chains on unsprung frames is 3/8 inch on primary chain and 3/4 inch on secondary chain. Magneto chain play should not exceed 1/4 inch.

The unusual threads, apparently non-standard tpi, used on many parts (i.e. the adjuster in the right-hand front fork leg for the brake cable has a thread of 1/4 inch diameter and 24 tpi) are actually C.E.I threads. (Cycle Engineer Institute) Other known locations of 1/4 inch X 24 tpi CEI threads are the six clutch studs and special bottoming nuts, and the four bolts at the lower forks for attachment of front stand and forward mudguard stays.

The footrests are adjustable to two positions by removing & refitting on opposite sides. They are cranked and can be set in front, or behind, their fixing point.

The wheel hub taper rollers bearings (Triumph P/N 6347) are no longer available. (Tapers have been shallower since 1946.) The originals were nine-roller taper bearings with overall dimensions of 1 3/4 inches o/d, 1/2 inch i/d and 3/4 inch wide. They are stamped W5386.

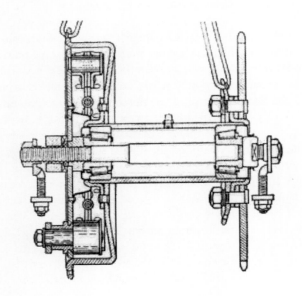

Rear wheel hub
showing the original
taper roller bearings.

The best option I have found in taper bearings was 1/2 inch i/d, 1 1/2 inches o/d, but with a width of only 17/32 inch. (P/No.s are 00050 for the cone and 00150 for the cup.) A cheaper option is plain ball bearings. (Taper bearings are needed where there is a side load but there is none with a wheel, and Triumph only used tapered for adjustment purposes. Bikes today use plain bearings.) The closest option there is 1/2 inch i/d, 1 5/8 inches o/d and width 5/8 inch. (P/No. is MJ 1/2 - MJ half.) It should be easy to turn up something for the outside to bring the diameter up an 1/8th inch and the side would require a packing spacer also of 1/8th inch thickness. Be sure that this spacer is turned to apply the full 1/8th inch to the centre of the bearing, and with a clearance for the bearing outer to allow the bearing to rotate with the wheel - otherwise you'll lock the whole thing up!

Somehow the Instruction Booklet fails to mention that it is necessary to move the rear mudguard and carrier assembly back about 3/4 to 1 inch in order to remove the rear wheel! This is so that the rear wheel may be moved back sufficiently to drop from the frame lugs. (This also means disconnecting the rear brake rod which passes through the rear mudguard.) In order to disconnect the rear carrier from the frame the studs which pass through the lower carrier lug need to be removed. As these studs also join the two rear frame sections it is a good idea to have the machine supported at the footrests. Otherwise, if supported on the rear stand, or wheel, with the studs removed all weight is transferred onto the single horizontal rear frame member and there is the risk of it fracturing. To facilitate removal of these studs it is a good idea during restoration, or when the studs are otherwise removed, to file two flats on the last 1/4 inch so that a spanner can be used to wind them in and out.

Because of the tendency for the main silencer to burn through at the lower front, where the gases are suddenly turned through near 90 degrees it is a good idea if having a replacement made to have a thickish steel plate welded internally at that point so that the gasses are turned off a 45 degree angle.

27 X 2.75 tyres equate to 21 X 2.75 in modern terms, and are very difficult to find. Suitable replacements are 21 X 3.00, block pattern, used by some oriental machines of the 1970's & 1980's.

Tyre Pressures

⇨   Solo - 18 lbs Front, 21 lbs Rear
⇨   Combination - 20 lbs Front, 25 lbs Rear, 18 lbs Sidecar

Patent Numbers

- Carburettor — Pat. No. 24213/14
- Mechanical pump/oil feed adjuster — Pat. No. 244018
- Fuel tank hand-pump with oil-feed tap — Pat. No. 268985
- Gearchange mechanism — Pat. No. 237461
- Enclosed kickstart mechanism — Pat. No. 243851
- Gear selection-rod buffer — Pat. No. 249972
- Throttle/air and advance / retard control levers — Pat. No. 191457
- Fork friction damping disks — Pat. No. 226017
- Front brake — Pat. No. 278525
- Rear brake shoes — Pat. No. 186422
- Footrests — Pat. No. 240300
- Brooks Supple Seat — Pat. No. 218762

Spares Sources

To aid owners, below is a starting list for spares. As this can never be comprehensive or up to date, it is recommended that the reader contacts one of the many veteran or vintage motorcycle clubs across the world. There are also currently many active social networks, an example being Facebook, and these can be an ideal place to gain opinions and hear what other people have tried.

- Bearings - Phil Haywood at The Vintage Bearing Company, www.vintagebearings.co.uk
- Brake material - Vintage Motor Cycle Club, UK, vmcc.net
- Footrest Rubbers - Jeff Hunter Engineering
- Kickstart Spring - Paul Savage, Sambourne, Worcester
- Mudguards - Michael at Vintage Steel, enquiries@vintagesteel.com.au
- Paint - Craftmaster Paints, www.craftmasterpaints.co.uk
- Spark Plugs - The Green Sparking Plug Company www.gsparkplug.com
- Transfers (Headstock and tank)
  - Classic Transfers Ltd., www.classictransfers.co.uk
  - VMCC, Burton- on-Trent
- Tyres - Vintage Tyre Supplies, Beaulieu www.vintagetyres.com
- Main Silencer Box - Willem Pol, Holland. (Cast alloy)
- Pistons - JP Pistons of Adelaide, South Australia. Part No. JP 1099
- Valve Cap Washers - Robin James, Leominster

Please note that inclusion or exclusion in this list does not imply any endorsement. There is also no guarantee that the organisations listed will have availability of items or that the organisation continues to exist.

Performance Figures

Model N

Comfortable cruising speed 40mph.
A 35-year owner quotes approx. 70mpg, and a top speed of 56mph against a car speedometer.

Model QA

Triumph claimed 60-65 mph with the "specially tuned QA without constant tinkering and attention". (That was the 1926 version of the Model QA so the 1927 version would be similar or better.)
A 1926 Model Q lapped Brooklands at over 73 mph.

Model NP

This would be similar to the Model N.

Literature

Instruction Book

▭   Models N and QA. (Also use for the Model NP)

Parts List

▭   Models N & QA. (1927)
▭   Models NP & N de Luxe (1928)

The above items are obtainable as photocopies from the Vintage Motor Cycle Club in Britain.

Announcements

▭   Models N and QA - The Motor Cycle, September 9th, 1926
▭   Models N and QA - Motor Cycling, September 29th, 1926
▭   Model NP - The Motor Cycle, September 22nd, 1927

Road Test

There were no road test of the Models N, QA-2 or NP.

Controls

Time now to acquaint yourself with the controls - and get on the road!

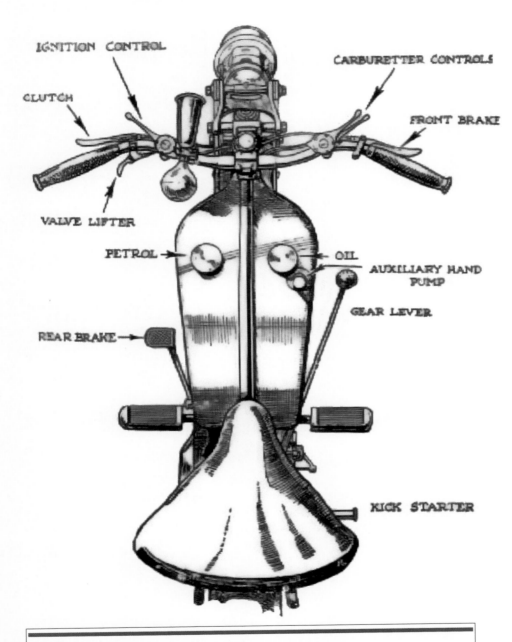

IGNITION CONTROL

CARBURETTER CONTROLS

CLUTCH

FRONT BRAKE

VALVE LIFTER

PETROL →

← OIL

AUXILIARY HAND PUMP

GEAR LEVER

REAR BRAKE →

KICK STARTER

NOTE – This diagram is actually of the 277cc Model W. However, controls for the Models N, QA and NP are the same apart from the hand pump which is further in from the edge of the tank. With a twist-grip throttle a twin-lever on the left controls air and magneto.

Surviving Machines

I have currently identified Models N, NP and/or QA-2 still surviving in Australia, Brazil, Britain, Bulgaria, Canada, Holland, Nepal, New Zealand, South Africa, Southern Rhodesia (Zimbabwe) and Switzerland.

Whitely Sidecars

The two-seater passenger body with safety-glass windscreen and canvas hood, towed by a 1927 Model N

In 1927 and 1928 the firm of Whitley Sidecars, London Road, Coventry, manufactured trailers for towing behind solo motorcycles using their Patented stabiliser coupling. Being a Coventry company it was perhaps natural that the motorcycles used in their advertisements were also Coventry made.

The commercial van-body trailer for local deliveries - "Car space with motor cycle economy". In this advertisement the tow vehicle is a 1928 Model NP

About the Author(s)

Something about the author - Peter Cornelius.

Peter's motor cycling days started in August 1955 with the purchase of a Triumph Tiger Cub. Peter was at this time in the Royal Air Force and had actually only learnt to ride a two wheeled pedal bicycle nine months earlier, at the age of 19! Having learnt the pleasures of the open road, the sight of a 200cc Ariel Colt and a 199cc Triumph Tiger Cub in a dealer's window prompted the decision to obtain a machine with an engine. The Cub looked delicate next to the Colt but memories of pillion riding behind a colleague, who illicitly kept his Cub in a farmer's barn while both served as RAF Radio Apprentices, made the decision easier.
So started a lifetime interest in the Triumph.

A later bike, a 1958 Tiger 110, was sold in order to settle into married life and a return to two wheels was not prompted until the fuel crisis of the early 1970s. Naturally Triumphs were the mode of transport and interest then leant towards earlier machines.

A personal challenge to break the dating code/s of machines manufactured after 1923 (Triumph's records were lost with the factory during an air raid on Coventry on the night of 14th November, 1940), prompted research into the variations of individual Triumph models over the years and subsequent delves into the social history which initiated the production of certain models.

Peter Cornelius, the author, ready for a run on his trusty 1927 Triumph Model P, and always willing to help every person with their early Triumph motor cycles

As Marque Specialist for Triumphs manufactured between 1920 and 1933, of the Vintage Motor Cycle Club based in Britain, Peter was recognised as a world authority on Vintage Triumph motor cycles. He continued to widen his knowledge and researches to cover all pre-1940 machines, following on from his early retirement in 1993 and subsequent emigration to New Zealand.

In July 2021, just before his 86th birthday, Peter made his final ride on this earth. We only hope that "the Triumphs of God" are now getting as much help from Peter as so many of us did over several decades.

Something about the custodian - Richard Cornelius

Richard being the son of Peter Cornelius, gained the motorcycling bug early in his life and can still remember the thrill of travelling pillion on his dad's 1956 Triumph Speed Twin (and the vibrations). From 13 he was lucky enough to learn to ride for himself on his uncle's farm and when he was 15, went and purchased a non-running, 1955 Triumph Tiger Cub for £50 and, together with his father, Peter, completely stripped and restored it over the following couple of years.

On becoming custodian and curator for the books, Richard is taking the opportunity to update the series for the future generations including respectfully re-writing of each book individually, with the intent and aim that people will be able to easily purchase theses where, and how they want, including traditional print, digital e-book, online retailers, book stores and libraries.

Richard would love to hear from you, your experiences of early Triumph motor cycles, and model details to continue his father's research. Contact details are on the website, www.earlytriumph.com (formally Peter's original site at www.triumph.gen.nz)

Still riding into his 80's, here's Peter and Richard out for a run together on Richard's original 1955 Tiger Cub and Peter's favourite Triumph, the 1927 Model P

Researching "The FACTS"

Across the period from the early 1980's until his passing in 2021, Peter Cornelius conducted original research with the original intent of being able to identify and accurately date every pre-1941 Triumph motor cycle. This entailed having to identify the differences for every model throughout their long production, plus the differences for the countries they were sold in.

Along with this Peter also identified additional details that have never previously been documented even in the manufacturer's literature.

Identifying complete surviving machines

A significant source for this research was to identify as many surviving machines and major spares as possible so that the real machines that were built could be determined, so that inaccuracies in advertised details could be discounted, as could any potential modifications by the numerous owners.

All the details during the research, details of owners and machine specifics, was and is, kept strictly confidential.

Confirming specific components

Specific details from these machines and spares included all, or some of:

⇨ Engine number (including any preceding or following letters)
⇨ Frame number (including any preceding letters)
⇨ Gearbox number (including any letters)
⇨ Registration number (though only UK registrations were later found to be of any useful significance)
⇨ Original Registration Date, if known
⇨ Any known machine history or particular machine information
⇨ Detailed photographs

Researching documentation from the period

For documentary evidence Peter identified and obtained the original documents, or copies, (and is also detailed in the section Literature for your benefit)

⇨ Original Triumph documentation, manuals, and spare part lists, for every model and year
⇨ The autobiography of Siegfried Bettmann, the founder of Triumph (an extremely rare 5-volume set)
⇨ Newspapers, magazines, and books from the same era as the models
⇨ Modern documentation was also read avidly, though not as an original source of information since it had already been identified that these sources could be inaccurate and the same inaccuracies copied by multiple authors

Surviving early Triumph motor cycles have been identified in:

The depth of the research is highlighted by the number of owners that Peter had been in contact with and the countries and continent he had touched. Below is the list of 51 countries that Peter had identified surviving early Triumph in.

⇨ Argentina	⇨ Lithuania
⇨ Australia	⇨ Luxembourg
⇨ Austria	⇨ Malawi
⇨ Belgium	⇨ Malta
⇨ Brazil	⇨ Nepal
⇨ Bulgaria	⇨ Netherlands
⇨ Canada	⇨ New Zealand
⇨ Chile	⇨ Norway
⇨ Croatia	⇨ Poland
⇨ Cyprus	⇨ Portugal
⇨ Czech Rep.	⇨ Romania
⇨ Denmark	⇨ Serbia
⇨ Eire	⇨ Slovakia
⇨ Estonia	⇨ South Africa
⇨ Finland	⇨ Spain
⇨ France	⇨ Sri Lanka
⇨ Germany	⇨ Sweden
⇨ Guernsey	⇨ Switzerland
⇨ Hungary	⇨ Tanzania
⇨ India	⇨ United Kingdom
⇨ Indonesia	⇨ U.S.A
⇨ Israel	⇨ Uganda
⇨ Italy	⇨ Uruguay
⇨ Jersey	⇨ Zambia
⇨ Kenya	⇨ Zimbabwe
⇨ Latvia	

Record your Triumph details

For completeness and to keep this edition true to the original book, although not relevant today, Peter always included a section for people to record their machines and parts, which then gave him yet more details to confirm his researches.

Your Triumph Model

Engine Number (with suffix letters) Date
Frame Number
Gearbox number

Spare Items

Engines (with suffix letters) Date
Frames
Gearboxes

Books in Triumph-The FACTS series

The FACTS series, by Peter Cornelius, was named due to a remark from someone whom Peter assisted with his restoration.

"Over the years many people have given me advice but you are the only one who has ever given me FACTS!"

The FACTS books on specific motor cycle models

Triumph 1901-1915, The Early Triumph Models (excludes Models H and LW) -
Note: originally published as a 2-booklet set
Triumph 1913-1926, Model LW (Junior, Baby)
Triumph 1915-1924, Model H and TT Roadster Model D
Triumph 1920-1927, Model SD (plus German Modell T and T II)
Triumph 1921-1928, The Racing Years, Ricardo and Horsman Triumphs
Triumph 1922-1927, Models R and IR
Triumph 1924-1927, Model LS
Triumph 1925-1927, Models P, Q and QA-1
Triumph 1927-1928, Models N, NP and QA-2
Triumph 1927-1929, Models TT and ST
Triumph 1927-1930, Models W de Luxe, W and WS
Triumph 1928-1929, Models N de Luxe and NL
Triumph 1928-1933, The Two Models NSD and the ND
Triumph 1929-1931, Models CO, RT and CTT
Triumph 1929-1932, Models CN and CSD (plus German TWN Modell T4)
Triumph 1930-1934, Models X, Z, Gloria, XO and XV/1
Triumph 1931-1933, Models WO, WA, WP and WL
Triumph 1931-1933, Models NM and NT, CA & CD
Triumph 1932-1934, Silent Scout Models A, B and BS
Triumph 1934-1936, The Val Page Models

The FACTS, for dating your machine - finally recreated since being lost in the 1940 bombing - and other information

Triumph 1901-1936, The Lost Records (and how to date early Triumphs)

The FACTS on the historic story of Triumph

The Triumph Story - part 1 1863-1906
The Triumph Story - part 2 1906-1912
The Triumph Story - part 3 1913-1919
The Triumph Story - part 4 1920-1928
The Triumph Story - part 5 1929-1934
The Triumph Story - part 6 1934-1940
- Note: these books may be republished as a single edition rather than the original 6-part set as shown.

Postscript letter from the editor and custodian, Richard Cornelius.

As the author's son, I'm the custodian of these books for the future generations. The words and images are almost entirely Peter's original works. I've mainly changed the formatting, cleaned up the images, with the purpose of amending as few words as possible, and if you'd met my father I hope you can still hear his voice as you read.

A request for feedback
Feedback is so very important to potential future readers and future generations, (plus I read them myself to improve the next book in the series to be published), and as such I would be extremely grateful if you could leave an unbiased reader review at the store you purchased it from (if you purchased online).

Kind regards
Richard Cornelius
www.earlytriumph.com

Printed in Great Britain
by Amazon

41467692R00027